More Than Four Walls:

The Ultimate Guide for Buying and Selling Real Estate in Dallas

By: Chastin J. Miles

© 2016 Chastin J. Miles. All Rights Reserved
ISBN 978-1-329-83326-5

Before You Read

This book was written based on my knowledge and past experiences. References or income examples of my business and/or the examples of others are not guaranteed. Your success is dependent on your application of the information presented. I highly recommend that you seek the assistance of a licensed real estate and/or mortgage professional before making your final decisions.

Contact Me

Chastin J. Miles

Rogers Healy and Associates

Phone: 214-589-0096

cmiles@chastinjmiles.com

chastinjmiles.com

Table of Contents

Chapter 1:

Everyone is Either a Buyer or Seller:
If You're Not, Then This Book is Not for You   8

Chapter 2:

I Was Intrigued by The Thought of
Owning a Business   18

Chapter 3:

Seller vs. Buyer: Getting Into the Mind of the Other
Party in the Sale   28

Chapter 4:

The Common Mistakes Sellers Make When
Trying to Get Their Home Sold   39

Chapter 5:

Make the Best First Impression or It May Be
Your Last Impression:
Ways to Create Love at First Sight for Your Home   51

Chapter 6:
How to Stage Your Home on a Budget　　67

Chapter 7:
What to Expect When Your Home
Is LIVE On the Market　　76

Chapter 8:
What to Do BEFORE You Buy a Home
in Today's Market　　85

Chapter 9:
How to Buy a House: The Basic Steps　　96

Chapter 10:
Can I Buy a House With No Money Down?　　104

BONUS Chapter 11:
How Much Money Do
Real Estate Agents Make?　　111

*"My Mission is to make a Positive Impact,
Not only in My Life, but in the Lives of Others"*
-Chastin J. Miles

CHAPTER ONE

Everyone is Either a Buyer or Seller:
If You're Not, Then This Book is Not for You

I'm pretty sure this is probably the first book that you have received from a real estate agent, so I want to start off by saying, Congratulations! The information obtained within this book will help you achieve success in your current or future real estate endeavors.

I wrote this book to not only give you valuable information but to give you confidence in buying or selling a home in Dallas, Texas.

Real estate transactions are significantly different from those of previous years. Therefore, you need current, up-to-date information to assist you in making effective decisions in this market.

After reading this book, or the *content* presented, you should find yourself equipped with the basic tools to continue enhance your experiences.

If this is your first real estate transaction, Congratulations!

If this is your second,
third,
fourth,
fifth, ... or even tenth real estate transaction,
Cheers!

Media coverage of the housing market crash in 2007-2008 sent the real estate market spiraling out of control.

Many refer to that time as the "bubble bursting" or "when the bottom fell out." Since then, the federal government and lenders have implemented changes with the intent of never having this type of crash happen again. Now, there are new documents, new laws, new interest rates, new everything!

There are so many changes that went on behind the scenes. I can tell you from a Realtors® perspective, lately, it seems like there's something changing every month!

With that being said, I hope to assist you in finding answers to the questions you have about real estate as you complete the reading of this book.

Have you guessed what I do? If not, let me share.

I work with people on a daily basis by helping them buy and/or sell a home in the Dallas/Fort Worth metroplex.

Over the years, as I continually work with people and understand their goals, I have concluded that it is my responsibility to help buyers save the most money or help sellers make the most money in their transaction.

If you're reading this book, you fall into one of those two categories.

Everyone is either a buyer or a seller.

If you are not, then this book is not for you and I encourage you to pass it to someone who it may be better suited.

If you DO want to save or make money *this is* the book for you.

You'll notice most of the chapters in this book have something to do with money in one way or another.

I'm going to cover the central message of money because hey, isn't that what real estate is all about? If you're selling a property you want to make money if you're buying the property you want to save money.

You want to get a deal, either way it goes, so that's why, I wanted to make sure I cover this topic thoroughly.

While you're reading this book I want you to have a pen and paper handy.

Why?

Because I'm sure there are going to be questions that come up and I want you to have those questions answered.

Write them down.

But, I want you to only present them to a licensed professional, like myself.

Again, write down all of your questions.

Also, in this book, there are a few activities that will require you to actually write them in the book. The reason I did this is because I feel that writing things down will help you remember them later.

Lastly, it will be good to reference them when you actually begin your real estate journey, whenever that may be. That way, you will have clear objectives of the things you need to focus on.

After you finish this book, contact me, or your licensed professional to discuss what you read.

My contact information is the back of this book. Feel free to use it.

I spent a good amount of time making sure I came up with valuable information for you.

Not all real estate professionals are the same.

Most agents can't provide you with *value*. I'll get into that a bit later.

Nonetheless, I want to make sure you are not missing any information when it comes to buying or selling real estate.

My decision to write this book is based on an experience I had in the past with a client.

Here's the story:

I received a lead email from a particular real estate website, back when they could be trusted a little bit, and I quickly called the prospect. She was an older lady and when we started working together, she made it very clear that this was not her first real estate transaction and she had a "clear expectation of the whole process."

Though her boldness made me nervous I knew it would be a smooth and easy transaction.

I did not cut any corners with her even though she informed me of her *well-versed in real estat*e background. I covered all of the same teachings and explanations that I offer all of my clients.

Luckily, she listened to everything I told her, even if she knew it or not. She also didn't correct me if she thought I was wrong.

I really appreciated her for doing that.

After the transaction was over, and we walked outside from the closing table, she told me, "I really like how thorough you are."

When she said that, of course I smiled and told her it was my pleasure. I was really just doing my job.

She began to tell me how most agents that she had dealt with in the past have never explained anything and have left her in the dark. She felt like she never knew what was going on *bad* or *good*.

This really bothered her.

Actually, it turns out the reason she chose me as the agent to contact was because of my videos that she had seen of me just explaining things on YouTube. Who would've thought she was on YouTube?

Who would of thought I would even be recognized?

She told me that if most agents took the time to educate their clients, real estate agents wouldn't have a bad reputation.

That was all I needed to hear, talk about a confidence boost.

After hearing her say that, I knew I wanted to educate everyone, whether they were my client or not.

I needed to come from a place of education when I work with people.

That's what the industry was missing.

Then I wrote this book, and you are reading it. It's because of one of my clients that you are reading this book, so thank her.

Real estate is my career and so I need to embrace it 100%. Some agents are just transaction based. They just care about closing deal after deal.

I am looking to create and build relationships.

I don't know if we will meet, but you taking the time to read this book is establishing a relationship. You will read about me and my real estate journey and you will also get a sense of how I work my business and the advice that I give my clients and my prospects.

As I said before, every agent is different. Every agent has their own style of marketing, teaching, working, and so on.

You wouldn't believe it but some agents sleep all day and party all night. Some agents close on one property a year. Some agents close on hundreds of homes a year.

It's not the most difficult thing to get a real estate license. It is very difficult to make a lasting career out of this.

My story is unique and different from other agents. Once you know my story, you know me. You will understand how and why I am where I am today.

Hopefully, you will get a sense of my work ethic and what I believe.

This book will is the beginning of our relationship.

CHAPTER TWO

I Was Intrigued by the Thought of Owning a Business

I haven't lived in Texas my whole life. I moved to Dallas about a year out of college. I was born in Houston, you know, the big city down south?

My two brothers and I grew up as happy as we knew we could be.

We pretty much did all of the things normal kids do.

The only thing that was different about me is that I was intrigued by the thought of owning a business. As a young child, I always wanted to "create a startup."

At an early age, I experimented with creating and selling greeting cards, websites, and even clothes made out of newspaper. I guess you can say, I was a pretty creative individual.

During my freshman year of high school, I moved to a town north of Atlanta, Georgia, by the name of Alpharetta. This is where my interest in real estate truly began, although I didn't know it at the time.

Alpharetta was a very well preserved suburb of Atlanta. The town was well established and so was the real estate.

I loved riding around and seeing all of the big homes in the area.

It was actually a favorite pastime of mine.

I didn't know much about real estate but I was mostly intrigued by the design and architecture of the homes.

I looked forward to visiting the homes of my classmates so I could see the designs of the different homes.

Big homes, smaller homes, mansions and townhomes, they were all so different.

They each had their own personality.

I liked that.

Something I would notice while riding around is that many homes had the same builder but were somehow very different from one another.

It was as if they each were all custom-built. Which they may have been, I didn't know at the time if they were or not. It was just really cool, as a kid, to see how different they were.

It wasn't until I got to college that I was actually introduced to the real estate business.

I didn't study real estate or anything, actually *what had happened was*, sophomore year, my roommates and I decided to look for an off campus home to live in.

We wanted to be like all of the cool kids that lived off campus. We knew it would be amazing to have our own furniture and rooms. We were pretty much going to make our house the happening place!

Walking around campus one day, we saw a flyer taped to a door that was advertising rental homes.

It looked something like this:

OFF-CAMPUS RENTALS AVAILABLE NOW

Walk to campus. Close to restaurants and shopping. Perfect for roommates

3-4 BEDROOMS

$400 a month each

CALL :678-555-5555

livebyksurealty@hotmail.com

Our dream was about to become a reality.

This was exactly what we were looking for!

Since "I" was the smart one, of course, they made me call the number. Truth be told, I really didn't know what I was doing. I didn't know what I would say or what they would even ask me.

When I called, I spoke with a very nice lady who took all of my information. She asked me questions like:

"What are you all looking for in a home?"

"When were you all looking to move?"

"How many bedrooms do you need?"

…and maybe some other questions that I can't seem to remember.

I gave her the answers and she set up a meeting for us to come to her office.

The day of the meeting, well the next day, we were all super excited. We showed up to her office early and ready to get a house. Her office was really close to campus.

When we got there, it turned out to be a real estate office.

I'll never forget it.

It was in a red brick building in the far end of a grocery store parking lot. The name of the real estate company was big and red across the top.

We went inside but there was hardly anyone there. We got a little freaked out but still we wanted a house so we started exploring.

As we should have, right?

Luckily, she found us.

The nice lady sat us down and started having a conversation with my roommates and I.

While talking to her, I noticed some of the posters on the wall.

They were advertisements to become a real estate agent.

I was intrigued.

I think we may have been in some sort of a real estate classroom. We definitely weren't in her personal office.

During our conversation, she showed us a few homes on a television monitor, mounted to the wall, and asked which ones we wanted to see.

Really we wanted to see every one of them. Did I tell you how excited we were?

I could tell she wasn't feeling that idea. We ended up picking two homes that we liked.

She left the room and came back to say, "Ready to check them out?"

We jumped up like frogs in a pot of boiling water. We felt like adults. It was crazy!

She invited us in her car and told us not the mind the cigarette smell. Of course, we didn't care.

We hopped right in and she took us to the two homes and showed us around.

This was kind of fun. I was **hooked**!

I don't know if I was more hooked on the job or the idea of looking at homes.

I knew at that moment; this was something I wanted to hear more about. I didn't know the ins and outs of the business but I wanted in!

Long story short, we decided not to get the rental. Now that I'm an agent, and know the business, I feel a little bad about that. But! I did end up enrolling in real estate classes with their school about a week later.

I was in every class bright and early. I feel like I did very well in them. But, I ran out of money. Remember, I was a college student.

I didn't tell anyone in my family I was doing this. I was supposed to be at school getting my degree and I was skipping class going to real estate school.

So I dropped out of real estate school.

I will never forget, I told the instructor that I was going to come back after I got my degree and he told me "No you won't, that's what everyone says and they never do."

He was right, I didn't go back.

I didn't go back to that school anyway. It wasn't until 3 years later that I enrolled in real estate school again, this time though, I was doing it in Texas. My native land.

I was focused and I knew I was going to get my license the second time around.

I still didn't know the ins and outs of the business but I wanted it. The little voice in my head just would not let me quit.

I took my courses again here in Texas and passed my state exam.

The rest of the story is still in progress.

Today, I'm extremely happy that I made that decision. Having a career in real estate has taught me so much.

This is a business that allows me to use all of my talents all the time. Yes, there are ups and downs, lots of them. But still, at the end of the day, I love what I do.

I appreciate you taking the time out to read this book. I want you to learn something from it. I've spent months writing this.

I'm going to tell you up front, this is my first book. It won't be my last, but I had to start somewhere. I like reading. When I read books, I always try to learn something from them. When I wrote this, I wanted to make sure I was teaching something.

My story is by no means complete.

In my eyes, this is only the beginning. You are a part of my beginning.

That's enough about me, now it's time to get into what this book is supposed to be about.

CHAPTER THREE

Seller vs. Buyer:

Getting Into the Mind of the Other Party in the Sale

"In a negotiation, we must find a solution that pleases everyone, because no one accepts that they must lose and that the other must win... Both must win!" — *Nabil N. Jamal*

I never told anyone this but when I was in college, I changed my major about once a semester. I've taken all types of classes. I've always had fascinations with different subjects. I have taken business classes, marketing, language, culinary arts, and even psychology.

Psychology was actually one of my favorites. It was very interesting. It was interesting to be taught about the capacity of our mind and how powerful it is.

The mind literally can change an outcome.

I'll never forget the line from David J. Schwartz, the author of *The Magic of Thinking Big*.

He says:

"Believe it can be done. When you believe something can be done, really believe, your mind will find the ways to do it. Believing a solution paves the way to solution."

I tell myself this over and over again. It can be applied in so many areas of life, including real estate. Not just for a real estate agent, building a business, but also for the buyer or seller participating in the transaction.

We must understand each other's minds and the way the other party thinks when it comes to the transaction.

When it's time to begin negotiating, Realtors® often use the term *win-win*. You may hear it on one of those real estate television shows.

What this means is that, at the end of the transaction, both parties are winning in some shape or form. This is a common term used in real estate. It's a win for everyone.

At the end of the day, to make a transaction work, both parties must agree.

Now the *not so easy* part is getting to the win-win.

A seller cannot get a home sold without a buyer and a buyer cannot purchase a home without a seller.

Basic common sense right?

It's like that concept of supply and demand. I believe I learned that in an economics class in middle school.

I named this chapter Seller vs. Buyer.

The reason I did this is because most of the time both parties in the transaction are thinking this way. It's very rare that the sellers think in terms of the buyer and a buyer thinks in terms of the seller.

Each party is out for their own good. Real estate transactions can get a bit messy. Luckily, there are agents in place that act as mediators to get both parties to a reasonable conclusion so everyone can move forward.

I often encourage both parties to think about the other side, especially when it comes to negotiation.

Now don't get me wrong, my duties and obligations lie with whichever party I am representing in the transaction.

Nonetheless, we can all have a smoother transaction if we work together instead of work against each other. A reasonable interest for everyone can be met, if it's done correctly.

I would say, 90 percent of the time, the seller wants to *Net* the most money. This means, after the transaction is finalized, the seller wants to take away as much money as possible.

Each seller has their own reasons for wanting this. This could be to pay off a mortgage, pay for repairs, debt, who knows… and often times, the buyer will never find out.

Just know, the person selling the home, wants to walk away with something. Unfortunately, this is not always the case.

Sometimes a seller may not *net enough* to even pay off the mortgage.

Net = sales price – all of the seller expenses

In this case, they may have to bring money to the table. Sometimes they could just break even.

I have seen situations before when I seller has had to bring a substantial amount of money to the closing table just to sell the home. The other party in the transaction didn't find that out until the end. But still, it happens.

If you are the one buying the home, oftentimes you may not even know why the seller is selling. Therefore, you just take it as they want to make money.

Hey, isn't that a big reason why we invest in real estate anyway?

On the other side, buyers want to make sure they are not overpaying for a property.

You can even say, buyers want to make sure they are "getting a deal".

In the market that we have experienced during the past few years, specifically meaning the last 2 years, there hasn't been many *"deals"* here in Dallas/ Fort Worth to speak of, so buyers just want to make sure they are making the right decision, especially when it comes to spending money.

We are in a market where homes are selling very quickly. Multiple people are trying to win the same home. I tell buyers, getting a deal today, is getting an offer accepted.

For first time buyers, the thought of spending hundreds of thousands of dollars on a home is a bit frightening. They just want to make sure they are making the right decision.

From offer to closing, there are a few opportunities for negotiation. During the negotiation opportunities, everyone's true motives often show themselves. It's kind of funny, but not so funny, if you ask me.

First, there's the offer.

The offer makes a statement and lets the seller know what exactly the buyer is *thinking* the property is worth and what they are willing to pay for it.

This is the first period that everyone will go back and forth until a true meeting of the minds happens. We can't move forward until everyone accepts all of the terms set forth.].

What you negotiate before the offer is accepted can be pretty much anything.

The most common areas of negotiation are sales price, closing costs, and closing date. It's in those areas that the numbers mostly fluctuate when a negotiation is happening. There are other little things like home warranties, furniture, and title policies, but I won't get too technical right now.

Moving on, the next time for negotiation is during what's known as, the option period. The option period is after your offer has been accepted.

During this option period, the buyer has the option to purchase the home or terminate the contract, no questions asked. Before the option period is complete, the buyer will most likely conduct an inspection by a licensed inspector. When the inspection report is generated, typically, the buyer and seller will negotiate again on anything that appeared in the inspection that the buyer and inspector *thinks* is a concern.

The reason this is a negotiating factor is because buyers, often times, want the sellers to either complete the repairs, put up some money, or take some money off for the repairs to be completed; and by "take off money", I mean off the sales price.

Just to let you know, when a buyer sees an inspection report with issues, big or small, it creates panic in their minds.

In the buyer's mind they are seeing: hazards, dangers, obstacles, and most importantly, money. Money that they will need to spend to make everything right.

It's not uncommon for a buyer to *think* that a home is falling apart just from an inspection report.

I've had this happen many times with a number of my clients, especially my first time home buyers.

It's perfectly normal.

Just imagine if you were going to purchase a home, or let's use the example of a car, and you saw a CarFax® report that showed lots of things that you wished weren't on there, wouldn't you be hesitant on making that purchase?

If you understood that, you have now entered into the mind of a buyer.

Now, I'm not saying that just because that's the way a buyer thinks, then you should automatically do what they say. I am saying, there needs to be a mutual agreement.

If you are able to take care of some things, take care of them.

If you are on the buying side, be reasonable to your sellers. The sellers are *not* your servants and **NEED** to be treated like an equal party in the transaction.

You should consider allowing the sellers to take on things that you know you would not be able to handle after the transaction is completed. I would also take into account things that may be unsafe in the home. If there are electrical, plumbing, roof, foundation, or other major issues, then yes, by all means request them.

If something is as simple as adding a light bulb, or replacing a light switch cover, I think you can handle that. If you can't, I probably shouldn't look into purchasing a home at this time.

Changing a light bulb definitely won't be the hardest thing you will probably have to do.

Buyers that get too picky **can lose** a really good home.

Sellers can say no to anything that you ask. It's totally up to them whether they would like to repair something or not. When it seems like a buyer is nitpicking or being unreasonable, a seller may not put up with it.

The key to all of this is to work together.

Get into the minds of each other and think what they can be thinking. It's not a good idea for one party to think that the other party is being very unreasonable. That's how transactions blow up and fall apart.

It's no fun for anyone involved, including the realtor, loan officer, Title Company, and whoever else may be working on the transaction.

CHAPTER FOUR

The Common Mistakes Sellers Make When Trying to Get Their Home Sold

Selling your home is a complicated process, and you could encounter numerous issues along the way that may throw the transaction off track. But if you're equipped in advance, with some savvy know-how, you'll be prepared for potential complications—which will go a long way toward making your home-selling experience smooth and trouble free.

Luckily, the role of an agent is meant to make things a lot easier for everyone involved. I want to take this opportunity to share with you some of the common mistakes that sellers make when selling their home.

I came up with this list from experience. I see these things happen all the time. Not just with me but with other agents as well.

The first mistake I often see sellers making is **choosing an agent for all the wrong reasons.** Getting your home sold for the most money possible, and in the best time frame possible, is a huge job that could affect you for years to come.

With that in mind, choosing a real estate agent because she's your neighbor or your sister-in-law could be a very bad idea. I'm sure your sister-in-law is a great lady, but all homes are different.

I tell people this all the time. If I'm making cold calls to try and help homeowners sell their home, I always ask them, "what made you choose your last agent?" Some of the answers I get you wouldn't even believe. You would think some people were giving me their whole family tree that led them to their last agent.

Recently, a friend of mine referred a couple to me. Before she gave me their information, she felt the need to "prep" me for what they had been through. I'm actually glad she did this so that I would know what I was getting myself into.

It turns out this couple had tried to sell their home for the previous six months. They were not successful.

They didn't feel like it was the agents fault, they thought that it was just a bad market for their home. Six months had gone by since their home was taken off the market, and now they were selling their home *by owner.*

For those of you who don't know what that means, basically, this time, they were trying to sell the home themselves without an agent.

When my friend gave me their information, I immediately called.

Really, all it took was one call from me, and they were ready to sign a listing agreement. They had every intention of selling and moving on with their lives.

The agent they chose was a friend of their family. They felt an obligation to list their home with this friend. When it didn't sell, instead of blaming the friend, they blamed the market.

Well needless to say, everyone knew we were in one of the hottest real estate markets ever to hit North Texas.

I asked them to provide me with some of the marketing pieces the agent placed in the home, guess what? There weren't any, no surprise to me.

Next, I looked up the listing from the last agent, but I decided against sharing the information with the home owners. I didn't want to offend them or cause any tension in their friendship.

You wouldn't believe what I saw.

The photos looked like they were taken with a camera phone, *which you'd be surprised how many agents do that*. The property description did not read like any property that I wanted to see.

There were misspelled words, incomplete driving directions, the whole nine yards! As an agent, I couldn't believe it. I know if the homeowners had seen this, they would have instantly gotten angry. It was marketed at such a hindrance to them.

I could have used that to my advantage, but it's not my style to bad mouth another agent.

I've come to realize my level of service isn't the same for everyone. It's not okay, but it is what it is. Just to shorten this story, in less than a month, we were at the closing table.

The property had been properly listed and marketed. We got the right buyer, well to be honest, multiple buyers. Today, she raves about my services.

I have told her over and over, it's all in the right agent. I can't stress this enough.

You will waste time and money working with the wrong agent. I'm all about friends and family, but hold them to the same standards that you would hold me or any random agent. If this had been any other agent, they would have probably fired them.

I don't want you to think that their previous agent was trying to be malicious, that was probably not the case. The fact of the matter is, not every agent is the right agent for the job.

If I came in for a listing appointment, you would probably ask me the same questions most sellers ask.

How long have you been in real estate?
How many homes have you sold?

How long does it take your listings to sell?

You know it's true.

With that being said, hold them to the same standard you would hold an agent that isn't a friend of the family.

The next mistake sellers make is to **hire an agent just because he or she promises to sell your house for more money than other agents**—it's a common strategy for some agents to overinflate the projected selling price just to get your listing.

What that does is it leaves you with your house on the market for much longer than it should have been; you'll just end up dropping the price until it's finally at the price it should have been in the first place.

As agents, we can't really tell you what your list price should be. We can provide statistics, facts, and recommendations but you have the final call.

If you have made the decision to hire an agent to sell your home, don't make the job harder than it has to be.

Our expertise and market knowledge will provide you with a price recommendation. It's often the sellers' greed that will cause a listing to sit on the market and go stale.

It would be nice if you could price your house based on how much you'll need to buy your next house, pay all your relocation expenses, and maybe with enough left over for a nice weekend in the Bahamas, but it just doesn't work that way.

You **can** control the asking price, but you **can't** control the selling price—the market does. And if you price is too high—it will cost you more in the long run.

Overpriced homes languish on the market and tend to end up selling for less than homes that were priced at market value from the beginning.

Are you familiar with how this could happen?

Basically what happens is, buyers agents will advise their clients on which homes are good deals and their clients will listen.

If there are 3 homes for sale in your neighborhood and 2 of them are priced right, those two will most likely get most if not all of the offers. The overpriced home may not even get as many showings for it because buyers and agents know the home is overpriced. If you do get offers, you may consider them "lowball" compared to what you are asking.

On the other hand, the homes that were priced right oftentimes experience multiple offers that will drive the final selling price up.

Once you decide to sell, you need to detach yourself from the house and view the transaction strictly from a business standpoint.

Don't get offended if someone makes a low offer or doesn't show appreciation for all those *special home improvements* you've made over the years. Once it sells, it will no longer be your home and none of those things will matter. Remember the previous chapter when I said to think like a buyer? This is one of those instances as well.

It's also important to **be upfront with buyers about defects in the house**. Here in Texas, we have a disclosure form, and it can help prevent a lot of trouble (and lawsuits) down the road if it's used properly. Buyers tend to view a defect less negatively if it's disclosed by the seller before it's discovered by their home inspector or in the worst case, after they move in.

Once the home inspector says it's a problem, sirens and red flags go off in the buyer's mind. Remember me referencing to that earlier? Be smart about this. **Disclose, disclose, disclose,** no matter how bad it may be.

Lastly, **be careful of unqualified buyers.** In the excitement over finally having a buyer for the house, many sellers jump at the first one who comes along.

If that "buyer" hasn't been properly pre-qualified for a mortgage, you may lose months of valuable time while the buyer tries unsuccessfully to obtain a mortgage. Don't sign a contract until the buyer has been pre-qualified (including a credit check) by a trustworthy, legitimate lender.

For the most part, I prefer to work with local lenders from mortgage companies here in the Dallas/Fort Worth area.

A buyer can really obtain a mortgage from anywhere.

It's their choice.

There are lots of companies out here advertising lowest rates, simple "online" application, or a fancy TV commercial with a catchy jingle. They attract lots of buyers. This isn't always a good thing. Something I do for my clients is really try to pre-qualify a buyer, even if I'm the listing agent.

Selling a home is rarely easy and it can be emotionally challenging, but you don't have to let it make you crazy. By avoiding these common seller mistakes, you can save yourself weeks or months of valuable time and help ensure a smooth transaction and a positive outcome.

CHAPTER FIVE

Make the Best First Impression or It May Be Your Last Impression

Ways to Create Love at First Sight for Your Home

"You never get a second chance to make a first impression." **-Harlan Hogan**

It's true in relationships, and it's also true in real estate. The impression that your home gives to potential buyers the first time they see it, isn't just important- it's absolutely critical to selling your house for the most money possible.

Here are five ways you can make sure it's a case of love at first sight when buyers visit your home:

1. Increase curb appeal.

We're not supposed to judge a book by its cover, but people judge houses by their exteriors all the time. Make sure that yours looks its best by putting all the toys and tools where they belong, keeping the yard mowed and bushes trimmed, and touching up or repainting any doors and trim that need a lift.

Even a new welcome mat and front door hardware are inviting and give the house a well-cared-for appearance. If there are any areas on the exterior that may need a little touch up paint, take care of that ahead of time.

I like to take it a step further, if you are selling in the fall or winter and there are leaves everywhere, get those cleaned up. If your exterior fence is in bad shape, get that taken care of. There have been so many backyards with the fences lopsided or falling apart.

That does not show the beauty of your home.

Lastly, if there are cobwebs around the entry way, get rid of them.

Just think about this, when an agent is showing a potential buyer, they are all most likely standing at the door while the agent is getting it unlocked. With that minute of idle time, the buyer is looking around.

I've even had buyers not want to go into a home just by the way the front yard looks.

Yes, this really happens. I wouldn't have put it in this book if it didn't.

2. **Stage the interior.**

You want potential buyers to picture themselves living in the house (not you), so make it easy for them. Box up any of the stuff you don't need and move it to the garage or better yet, get a rented storage unit. Take out half of what's stored in all the closets and neatly arrange what's left. Closets can get messy but they shouldn't be overlooked.

Remove family photos, distracting knickknacks, and every bit of clutter.

I tell sellers all the time **de-clutter, de-clutter, de-clutter**.

De-cluttering includes, books, papers, excessive décor, toys, and pretty much anything that may crowd a room. It's basically getting it out of there.

Touch up or repaint any walls that are scuffed or are painted in non-neutral colors. Loud wall colors are very distracting. It may have worked for you, or your children, but it probably wouldn't work for the next buyer.

Also, some colors make rooms look smaller and more cluttered. Make sure that's not the case for your rooms.

A professional house cleaning is often an investment that will pay for itself many times over. And while you're at it, don't forget to have the carpets professionally cleaned if they look less-than-pristine. If not, you can almost guarantee a buyer is going to request the whole carpet be replaced.

3. Wash the windows.

This is something that a lot of sellers don't even pay attention to. Wash all your windows inside and out until they sparkle. This is one of those jobs that few of us like to do, but it makes such a difference in the overall appearance of your house. Dirty windows can make the nicest house look depressing and uncared-for. Think about if you were to look at a dirty window, how would that make you feel about the home?

4. Fix what's broken.

There's no point in putting off repair jobs. Today's home buyers get home inspections, and your house's defects could turn into expensive negotiating points down the road.

You're better off going ahead and making any needed repairs now, so that buyers don't see little problems and wonder what other, bigger issues are lurking in the house.

I hope as you're reading this you're really thinking in the mind of a buyer, if so, this is for sure making sense to you. If you're still having a hard time, go back and read Chapter 3 again. Actually to make it easier, at the end of this chapter, I want you to do a home audit. I want you to take a moment and jot down any things that need to be fixed anywhere in the home. I've created a nice little list of common areas in the home that need repairs. This should help you when it comes time to getting those repairs done.

5. Get set for showings.

Make every showing appointment as appealing as possible. When you go to work in the morning, don't leave beds unmade or dishes in the sink- or that's sure to be the day a serious buyer wants to visit. (And you don't want to mess up on any qualified buyers, even if that means being ready to let your home be seen on short notice.)

If you do have a bit of notice before a showing, take a few minutes to turn on all the lights, put on soft music, and set the table. Little things can make a big difference!

You'd be surprised.

When you're in the midst of getting kids ready for school, going to work, and the myriad of other chores that go along with running a busy household, it's easy to lose sight of the little things that should be done to make sure your house sells for the most money possible. But keep in mind that you only have to do it for a short time, and if you do it right, you'll reap big rewards at the closing table for your efforts.

If you want to sell your house for the most money, you can't just leave it up to fate, or me, to make it happen.

In today's market, you need to do everything you can to make your house stand out from the crowd and attract the most buyers. I can give recommendations to my clients all day long but it's up to them to follow my lead.

So what can you do to make your home worth more money in the marketplace? Here are five smart projects you can do that will bring you more money at the closing table.

1.   Replace worn, damaged, or dated carpet.

I know I touched on this a couple of pages back. I want to make sure you really get how important it is. You may be tempted to offer the buyer a credit rather than go to the trouble of replacing carpets throughout your home, but if they need it and you're able to replace them—do it. Buyers aren't looking for credits; they're looking for nice houses that don't require lots of work.

The fact is, many buyers can't see past ugly carpet and won't even bother to make an offer on a house that has it. Replacing old carpet will make the house smell new and buyers will love it. Choose a neutral color such as a light tan or beige.

2.   Repaint the inside.

There's nothing like a fresh coat of neutral paint to make a house look brand new again.

If you can paint it yourself, it's a cheap fix that you can't afford *not* to do if it needs it. Again, many buyers have a very difficult time seeing past issues like unusual colors or scuffs and crayon marks on the walls.

If you have to hire someone to do it, it's worth paying to have it done-- or consider inviting a few friends over for pizza and painting party! You can always do the same for them when it's their turn to sell.

If you don't know what colors to choose, I recommend visiting your local paint shop and asking for recommendations. They are probably accustomed to working with builders and investors and even designers and know what's in season and know the definition of "neutral". If you paint colors are not up to date, get them updated. Even if it's appealing to you, a buyer may deem the whole house as outdated.

3. Paint or reface ugly kitchen and bath cabinets.

The kitchen and baths are two of the most important rooms to buyers, and if they look outdated, buyers will automatically overestimate the expense to update them.

You can make old cabinets look nearly new again by rolling on a coat of neutral, high-quality paint on them. Home improvement stores sell paints made especially for this purpose, and it's not difficult to do.

Alternatively, you may want to paint just the bases of the cabinets and replace the doors for a very reasonable cost.

Whichever one of these you decide to do, make sure it's done right. This needs to be a quality job.

I've seen some homeowners try this and it's been uneven coats of paint, half done shoddy jobs. My buyers walk in, and it's literally like an eyesore.

I remember when two of my clients, both first time home buyers, walked into this one particular home they were interested in. We opened the door where there was pink carpet everywhere. Yes, pink carpet! No offense if that's your carpet color now, but it was weird.

We had never seen anything like it.

When we got past the carpet and went into the kitchen, there was new granite countertops and what seemed like freshly painted kitchen cabinets. The appliances were outdated but luckily the updates they had done looked good. So we thought…

As we continued to look around, my client decided to open one of the freshly painted white cabinets. She opened it up and the inside was still the original color!

It looked horrible.

Then as she opened another cabinet, it fell off the hinge. This is definitely not something a buyer would want to see. I had to do some serious damage control to get them to look past that to see "the possibilities".

4. Update old-fashioned lighting.

If your home is sporting light fixtures from the 60's, or if they're just plain ugly, think about replacing them with some inexpensive new lights from the local home improvement store.

Attractive light fixtures and ceiling fans with light kits are available for well under $100, and they can quickly take years off your home's appearance. Make sure the lighting matches.

Be careful about using florescent bulbs in some rooms and LED or HD in others. Be consistent. It can come off looking cheesy.

5. Pressure wash the outside and add new mulch in the flower beds.

It's amazing what a difference pressure washing can make to the outside appearance of your home. If you rent a pressure washer and spend a day cleaning your outside walls, gutters, and walkways, you'll dramatically increase its curb appeal without spending much money.

For a few dollars more, buy a few bags of mulch and add it around trees and in flower beds. Remember reading about curb appeal a little while ago? Buyers have to be attracted to the outside before they'll bother looking at the inside.

Some buyers these days will do a drive by before they even call their Realtor® to show them the inside.

Don't let their impression of the outside ruin the real prize inside.

If you're trying to get the most money possible when you sell your house, it's important to make it look its best. Spending a few dollars and putting in some work now will pay off big at the closing table later.

Home Repairs Checklist

Take note of the repairs needed in your home

Area	Problem	Cost
Roof		
Foundation		
Walkway		
Exterior		
Sprinklers		
Electrical		
Plumbing		
Windows		
Appliances		
Floors		

Garage		
Walls		
Yard		
Lighting		
Vents		
A/C		
Toilets		
Sinks		
Shower		
Bathroom		
Cabinets		
Kitchen		

CHAPTER SIX

How to Stage Your Home on a Budget

A question I love to be asked by potential sellers is, "What do I need to do to get my home ready to be put on the market?"

It goes without saying that major issues like as a leaking roof or a cracked foundation need to be addressed. But beyond those major issues, what can you do to the inside of the home to really make a buyer want to put in an offer?

The one thing I always recommend is staging.

The best way that I can get you to understand staging is through this example.

Imagine that you are looking for your next home.

You walk into a house and see nothing.

By nothing, I mean, bare walls, bare floors, and empty rooms. How would that make you feel?

If you ask me, you would probably get a cold feeling. If you're not an interior designer, it would take you twice as long to imagine yourself in that home.

Now picture this, imagine walking into a beautifully decorated two story bungalow.

The walls were painted in a color that went very well with the freshly stained hardwood floors. You're walking around and you notice the furniture gives you the impression that you're in a French inspired villa. The artwork on the wall is modish yet inspiring.

You continue walking. The master bedroom gives you a chic and elegant feel, by this time, you're in love.

You see yourself waking up from a sound night sleep as the sun rises through the sophisticated drapes hanging in front of the window. You're happy.

Wake up!

Did that paint a clear picture for you? Well, that's staging. It's the art of making a buyer feel right at home through the interior design that you have been able to construct.

I'm sure with that example you probably saw thousands of dollar signs to make this happen. Well, the good thing is, it does not have to cost a lot of money.

You can stage a home on a budget and I'm going to help you. Here are some things you can do to give your home a nice staged look for buyers.

Clear the clutter. Clutter is the biggest distraction when it comes to a home.

All of the toys, furniture, fixtures, and miscellaneous things around the home combined, make up clutter.

When there's too much clutter, it often times can make your home feel small and uninviting. Getting rid of all the clutter is one of the biggest parts of staging a homeowner can do.

If there are items around the home that you don't use regularly, pack it up and get it out of sight.

It simply does not need to be there.

If you have no place to put everything, try the garage. No garage? Rent a storage unit or throw it away.

Your home probably won't be going unsold for too long if this is done right. Storages units are a cost effective way to hide the clutter. You can get one for as low was $30 a month. It's a practical investment you can make to get the home sold.

When you're getting rid of clutter, don't forget about the closets and cabinets.

Imagine if you were a buyer and you saw stuffed closets and bathrooms, you would end up thinking that there was not going to be enough storage for you and your belongings.

Therefore, make each space look bigger.

Next, **clean and polish the heck out of your home**. You want to give each and every buyer that steps through your door an impression that the home was well taken care of.

This is achieved through the cleanliness that presents itself. If you can afford it, hire a professional cleaning crew to come in and do a deep cleaning of everything. Most times, they will clean spaces you never knew could be cleaned.

If you don't want to hire anyone, buckle down and do the work.

Let no surface go untouched.

Be sure not to miss areas like baseboards, ceiling fans, and shelves. They collect dust pretty quickly and you may or may not have even noticed it.

Clean any areas on the walls and floors that have scuffs and spots. This is a really easy task you can do.

Get a magic eraser and scrub.

When you do this, you are giving buyers a cleaner more polished alternative to what they may currently have. They'll leave thinking "I'd rather live there than the dusty cluttered home I live in right now"

That's the goal.

Still with me?

Once that's done, it's time to **depersonalize**. All the years you've lived in your house; you have made it your home.

Got that keyword? *"Your Home"*.

When your home is for sale, buyers need to feel like it's *their* home.

I'm sure you have a beautiful family, but the buyer is not buying the home for your family. It's for their family, so take down your family pictures, and family air looms. Don't let them be a distraction or a deterrent.

Pack them up in a safe place. Besides, you wouldn't want a buyer to see all of that anyway.

Make everything in your home neutral. Just because you are a big fan of candy apple red walls does not mean everyone else is.

Imagine yourself going on a blind date. Unlike most experts recommend, your date enjoys every controversial topic out there. Politics, religion, money, you name it. You begin to notice; their views are totally opposite of how you feel.

After experiencing that, would you marry them? Probably not. It's the same way with a home.

Keep the conversation neutral. By conversation I mean the home. That way, no one will get turned off and they may actually see themselves with you in the future.

Lastly, **accessorize**. Now its time to make the home beautiful. If you've done all of the steps above, at this point, you're working with a blank canvas.

While you can do anything, take these cost effective recommendations.

Living Room - let items such as a pillow, rug, and a throw on the sofa do all of the work. They're simple but go a long way.

Kitchen - create a calming feeling with fresh flowers and a candle.

Bedrooms - make sure the bed is always made and you have a neutral bedspread. Remove your clothes, jewelry, and the treadmill in the corner, out of sight.

Bathrooms - hang a few towels that will compliment the walls. This is also a great place to have a single candle.

These are just a few tips.

I would also recommend hopping on Pinterest and looking at a few interior design concepts you can easily do.

If you have a little time on your hands, visit a new home community or an apartment community, in the area, and check out the model homes.

These are often times staged to sell and you can get some modern ideas.

When you're trying to sell, your mission is to make your home look as appealing as possible to as many buyers as possible—but you definitely don't have to spend a lot of money to do it.

CHAPTER SEVEN

What to Expect When Your Home Is LIVE On The Market

It's really happening now.

Putting your house on the market can seem daunting and nerve-wracking, but it doesn't have to be that way. I will be there to guide you and help you every step of the way.

Here are some of the things you can expect to encounter when you put your house on the market:

MLS. Once the paperwork is complete, your home will be placed in the Multiple Listing System (MLS) almost immediately. Well, give or take a few days. The MLS is a real estate database that allows other agents and buyers to see when your home is for sale. Over 90% of home buyers begin their search for a home online, so it's important that your home is listed in the MLS so it's easy for them and other Realtors® to find it.

The MLS will also syndicate to certain real estate websites. Here in North Texas, we have up to 5 days for the home to appear in MLS, unless otherwise stated in the listing agreement.

So, we don't have much time to play around.

Yard sign. You can expect a "for sale" sign to appear in pretty much the next day. I like to get this done immediately. Often, potential buyers cruise through neighborhoods they like, looking for homes that are for sale. It's also a great way to let other neighbors know the house is for sale- and you never know when one of them has a friend or relative that may be interested in buying your home.

Lockbox. When your home is on the market and we are ready for showings, I will install a lockbox on the door. This way, other agents can access the house for showings and you do not have to be available. At first, this may make you feel a bit uncomfortable, but it's important. If you don't have a lockbox, other agents will be more likely to put your home last on their list of homes to show, because it's a hassle to coordinate times for everyone to meet for a showing.

On the other hand, if you do have a lockbox, buyers agents can make an appointment to bring their buyers to see your house- even if you or myself aren't available.

Don't worry, random people do not have access to your home. Only a licensed professional will have access. I will still know who is showing the house, and agents should never show it without prior permission.

Luckily in DFW we have a showing service that we use. I like to use them to make things convenient for everyone and give my sellers piece of mind.

You will be notified of each showing including the day and time. As an added convenience, you can also be notified of the feedback from the other buyers and buyers agent.

Open houses. We will decide together whether an open house make sense for your particular situation. If we decide to have an open house, it will typically be open for several hours on a Saturday or Sunday.

It's best if you're not present for the open house, because buyers tend to feel uncomfortable and like they're imposing if the seller is there. You want buyers to feel comfortable opening closet doors and asking the agent lots of questions.

Showings. You're likely to get most of your showings in the first two to three weeks your home is for sale, but don't panic if it's not under contract by then.

30-45 days on the market is typical for many areas. If you get beyond 90 days without a contract, it's probably time for us to revisit the home's marketing and pricing strategy.

Nearly everything becomes easier once you know what to expect, and listing your home for sale is no exception.

Keep in mind that if you have questions or problems along the way, I will be there to assist you. By knowing what to expect and having professional help, you can avoid home-selling stress.

So, that happy day arrives when you come to an agreement with a buyer and your house is under contract. Now you can sit back, relax, and wait for the closing check to arrive, right?

Well, not exactly. There's still a lot of work to be done and hurdles to clear before the sale can be finalized, which typically takes about four to six weeks. Here are the most common events that will happen while you're waiting for closing day to arrive.

Buyer's Loan Approval. Ideally, your buyer will already be pre-approved by a lender at the time they contract on the house. This will save everyone time and effort, because they've already completed many of the steps necessary to get final loan approval.

Whether they are preapproved or not, there are steps that must be completed before final loan approval is obtained. If your home sale is subject to the buyer obtaining financing, it can be a bit nerve-wracking while you're waiting to hear whether they've obtained approval or not.

It's my responsibility let you know as soon as the buyer's loan approval is obtained, which usually takes about two to three weeks. If someone is paying cash for your home, none of that matters.

Home Inspections. The buyer will probably have a general home inspection performed, during which the inspector will check out your home's structure and systems to make sure they're in normal operating condition.

If the inspection shows that repairs are needed, and we negotiate a contract for the repairs, get estimates and have them completed before the buyer's final walk-through.

The buyer may also have other specialized inspections completed, such as those for pools, foundations, plumbing, and termite inspections.

Inspections are done during the option period. Remember I touched on that earlier? This is one of those times when negotiations can come up again. So be prepared.

Escrow and Title Work. An impartial third-party attorney or closing company, known as a Title Company, will get to work as soon as the contract is signed.

They'll order a title report, calculate the amount of the property tax that will be due on the day of closing, obtain a payoff amount from your mortgage company, and gather all the paperwork that's necessary to close.

They also act as a coordinator for the entire closing process, working closely with both the seller and the buyer to make sure that everything is in order.

The title company is also the one to issue the title policy for your property. Therefore, they will research your homes ownership, uncover any liens, pretty much resolve any issues that could cause problems for the new buyer when it comes to the title of the home.

Seller Responsibilities. As the home seller, there are a few things you need to do while you're waiting for the closing to happen. Provide any documents and contact information that the title company requests.

Keep your home maintained in the same condition it was at the time of contract, and be sure to keep your homeowner's insurance policy in full force through the date of closing.

As the closing nears, contact your utility companies to transfer service to your new place (but be sure to keep the utilities on at your old house through the date of closing; otherwise, the closing could be delayed if the buyers can't complete their final walk through). Be sure to set up a change of address with the post office before you move, as well.

The title company will notify you when the paperwork is done and coordinate a convenient closing date for you to sign all the final documents.

Once the closing day arrives and you have the proceeds in your bank account, it will finally be time to celebrate. All of the work of selling your home will be behind you, and you'll be able to move forward to your next adventure!

CHAPTER EIGHT

What to do Before You Buy a Home in Today's Market

The state of the real estate market is constantly changing. As agents, we can have a really good season, then a not so hot season. The state of our economy has many people wondering "when is the best time to buy a house?"

This is not bad, people are now more careful and that's definitely a positive. Do you remember back in 2008 when the housing market crashed? Many people were forced to sell their homes, even though they didn't want to.

Foreclosures were popping up all over the place and real estate agents were leaving the industry left and right. It was a really hard time for a lot of people. When that happened, it frightened many people.

Still to this day, many are wondering if it's safe, as they should.

When deciding to purchase a home many do not take the process lightly. Most only do it after careful and strategic planning. Buying a home is one of those big decisions.

Nobody really does it on impulse.

Have you ever visited a car dealership because you wanted to "look around?" I know I have. I looked around, I test drove, I drank their free sodas, and I walked out with a car. Going into the whole situation, there was something in me that wanted a new car. I needed a new car honestly.

When I spoke to a salesperson, everything just so happened to line up exactly how I needed it to.

The numbers were right, they were running an awesome special, and I must say, I'm pretty good at negotiating.

Well buying a home does not happen as quick but there are some similarities in the way to go about things.

Let's discuss those a bit.

Before I decided to even step foot in the dealership, I knew exactly what I wanted. I knew the make, model, and even color I wanted.

On a deeper level, I knew how much my insurance was going to be, how much gas would cost me to fill up, and how often I would need to take the car in for maintenance.

How did I know that? I did my research. That should be the first step with any big purchase.

Do your research.

When you begin to research the purchasing of a home, most importantly get educated. This is going to be a really big purchase for you. Therefore, education is key. Start to really understand how finances and credit work when you're beginning the process.

Before you attend an open house, learn about credit and finances. This is important because everyone's situation is different.

In actuality, just because you were approved for a credit card with a high limit, doesn't necessarily mean you'll get approved for a home loan. Loan officers and mortgage companies have different scoring systems when they are approving you.

If you are ready to look into your credit, start by requesting a copy of your credit report from AnnualCreditReport.com. You can get one free credit report per credit bureau every year.

Review the report, and make sure it's accurate.

You can also checkout websites like CreditKarma.com. Make a note of any accounts that are reporting negatively, and start working to improve them. This will guide you along the road to begin to raise your credit score.

A decent credit score is a necessity, especially when you are aiming for a good interest rate.

Once you know what your report contains, you can begin to work on it.

If you don't want to do it yourself, you can always speak to a mortgage lender and have them pull your credit.

Steer clear of any credit repair services or companies that promise you a high credit score.

I recommend that you speak to a real estate agent or lender before paying for credit repair services from a company that does not specialize in working with home buyers. It could cost you a lot of money.

The next thing you want to do before you buy a home is to review your budget. You need to know how much you can comfortably afford monthly and also up front down payments.

A big reason that many homeowners had to sell their homes in the past was because they simply couldn't afford them.

People purchased more than they could truly afford.

If your mortgage is going to be your only obligation, then that's great. Still consider how much of your income that the mortgage will consume.

Ask yourself, will I still be able to live my life after I pay my mortgage each month?

If the answer is yes, you're doing pretty good so far.

There's one more area you want to make sure you're prepared for the buying process.

Don't forget that there will be extra expenses involved in buying a house: closing costs, inspection fees, and so on. Make sure that you have enough of a cushion to cover these expenses. These expenses are aside from the actual down payment.

I will get into down payment amounts shortly.

Afterwards, you need to figure out what you realistically need in a home. This is going to be a little hard. It's easy for us to figure out what we want in a home, but not so easy to determine what we really need. Needs are the things that you cannot live without.

Sit down, open up the notepad on your phone and jot down your needs and wants. I would make a list of the thing you must have. After you finish that, you can make a list of the *"nice to have"* items.

I recommend you complete this list before you speak to a real estate agent (especially if you are buying a home with someone else).

I have a little questionnaire at the end of this chapter that can help you make a few decisions before you seek out an agent.

You will need an agent help you complete your transaction. When you go to purchase a home, you will sign lots of contracts and exchange lots of money.

You will need someone who is experienced in this field.

A good agent will really help you to understand what you're doing, beyond looking at homes. It can be very dangerous to not have someone working with you.

Although we are talking about agents, I won't just talk about me, *though I think I spoke about myself a bit in the previous chapters.*

You must take some time to do your research. Look for an agent with experience and a genuine track record with the ability to guide you through the process. Don't just choose any real estate agent. The person you attended high school with may have been a terrific classmate, however, your need for experience and know-how may not be met if he or she is not the right agent for you.

Ask others for referrals.

If the same name keeps popping up, in your area, then that agent is likely a good candidate to interview. **Or,** if you find yourself reading a book written by a real estate from an agent on how to buy or sell a home in Dallas, then you should definitely choose **HIM**.

Finally, you'll want to learn about mortgages, and get pre-qualified for a loan. Unless you are paying cash for a home, a mortgage is important. You want as much knowledge about this as possible.

Before an agent will take you out to see homes, they normally require a pre-approval for a mortgage. This can save both of you time by avoiding the touring homes that do not fit into your budget, plus you will need a pre-approval when it's time to make an offer. You don't want to do this last.

Let's say you find the perfect home that you want to move into ASAP, without a pre-approval, you can't make an offer. Someone can come right in after you, fully prepared, and get the home under contract.

In the end, you will be the one missing out because you weren't prepared.

Your real estate agent can often help you find a good mortgage professional (I have a few local ones I can refer you to).

Once you've done your homework and have a full understanding of everything, your home shopping experience will be enhanced by your knowledge and preparation.

I would like to purchase a home by:

_____

I would like my home located in:

_____

The reason I am deciding to purchase a home is:

_____

_____

_____

_____

My fears before starting the process are:

1. _____
2. _____
3. _____
4. _____

CHAPTER NINE

How to Buy a House: The Basic Steps

By now I'm sure you've noticed that there's much more to buying a home than visiting open houses or searching homes on websites.

You need to be knowledgeable of what's to come so that you don't make costly mistakes in the near future.

There is a good amount of preliminary work to do.

As mentioned in the last chapter, obtaining a strong pre-approval is included in the first steps. The lender you decide to work with will get that together for you. Who you work with matters, so again, do your research.

When it comes to a lender, you want to choose someone competitive, local, and experienced.

You also want someone you can trust.

The lender is going to need a good amount of personal information that you aren't used to giving out.

Be ready to provide documentation of work and income. This will include W-2's, bank statements, and also written statements of any income you have received in the past year or two.

Alongside your real estate agent, the lender will be an important person in this process.

If you need recommendations, I definitely have them for you. Each one is different and some specialize in specific situations, so it's best we find the perfect match for you.

The lender will have you initially fill out an application and provide some documentation to issue a pre-approval. Once we receive the pre-approval, then we will begin searching for homes.

This is where it gets fun.

Touring homes is fun but again, you must be serious and realistic. Although you may want a pool, sauna, and a rock climbing wall, but is that completely realistic for you?

You can have anything you want, if it fits into your budget.

Most budgets probably won't allow you to get EVERYTHNG you want, so it's important to prioritize.

I took a little time and put together a wants and needs list for you to fill out at the end of this chapter. Take some time and do that. It will make things easier when you are shopping.

As a matter of fact, stop reading now and take some time to complete the activity at the end of this chapter to bring your needs and wants into perspective.

Any decision makers need to be a part of this activity. That way, everyone is on the same page.

It could get a bit annoying to look at home after home after home. Your search would be more fun and effective by just looking at homes that truly fit your needs.

When you complete the activity, it would be a good thing to provide to your agent. Share the list you created with your agent. The agent can use the list to show you homes that best match your needs. This process will save many hours of travel for you and the agent.

During this time, listen to them. Don't try to view every home in a city or zip code.

Once your agent knows your wants and needs, hopefully they will do their job and only show you properties that fit your criteria.

Now, you've found a home and the offer you made is accepted (with the help of a Realtor®, like myself), get it inspected by a licensed home inspector.

The inspector will check the home from top to bottom—crawling in the attic, climbing the roof, testing the electrical systems, and giving it a good once-over to discover potential hazards or problems you could encounter.

Your agent can give you a recommendation for a good home inspector. Be careful though, this is one of those things that you get what you pay for. I've had some clients that want to hire an inspector because they are cheaper than all the others. Before you choose them for the job, know what you are getting.

The price of an inspection can vary by square footage of the home.

If you are needing a pool inspection, or termite inspection, those services would be additional.

Your home inspector should be licensed and qualified; Texas requires that the inspector is licensed as some other states do not.

Your real estate agent can assist in finding an inspector to meet your needs.

Please understand that there is no perfect home, however, you need to know what you are buying before signing the final documents.

After the inspection, you'll work closely with your lender to complete the mortgage process. There are lots of moving parts and steps during this time.

I could put them all in this book but then it would get lengthy and really boring.

The good thing to know is that an experienced agent will guide you through the whole process. This is something I go into detail more when I meet with a buyer to discuss the process. I like to give you a clear picture of what to expect during this time.

The important thing is to be conscious of timelines. Submit the paperwork requested by the lender immediately.

Deadlines are critical, and if you procrastinate, your loan approval will be delayed as well as your closing on the home. Avoid major purchases (car, television, etc.) during the waiting to close process- also, don't change jobs or overuse your credit cards. This is important.

Financial changes will raise red flags to the lender and could nullify your mortgage loan application. That includes opening new lines of credit.

Steer clear of that.

Application of these tips will assure that the home you buy will give you great satisfaction now and in the future.

House Hunting Checklist

Basic Requirements Minimum Bedrooms   1 2 3 4 5+

Minimum Bathrooms   1 2 3 4 5+

Minimum Size   _____ sq. ft.

Features (Circle must-haves, check nice-to-haves, and cross off things you don't want.)

Structural

- ☐ Garage (Min. doors: _____)
- ☐ Single Story
- ☐ Multiple Stories
- ☐ Basement

Interior Features

- ☐ Hardwood Floors
- ☐ Open Concept
- ☐ Granite Countertops
- ☐ Laundry Room
- ☐ Finished Basement
- ☐ Handicap Accessible

Location

- ☐ Waterfront
- ☐ City Views
- ☐ Quiet Street
- ☐ Cul-de-Sac
- ☐ Strong Schools
- ☐ Walking Neighborhood

Exterior Features

- ☐ Deck
- ☐ Porch/Sunroom
- ☐ Patio
- ☐ Pool
- ☐ Fenced-In Yard
- ☐ Hot Tub
- ☐ Shed
- ☐ Gardens/Landscaping

Heating and A/C

- ☐ Energy Efficient
- ☐ Central A/C
- ☐ Fireplace

Other

- ☐ _____
- ☐ _____
- ☐ _____
- ☐ _____
- ☐ _____
- ☐ _____

CHAPTER TEN

Can I Buy a House with No Money Down?

I get the question of programs for no money down very often. Is buying a home with no money down even possible?

For many people, home ownership seems out of reach because the money needed for a down payment or closing costs are not in the budget.

They can get quite expensive but vary on the purchase price of the actual home.

There are home loan programs that only require a minimum of 3.5% but the standard is 5% and up for many loans today.

When I'm driving in my car, or watching TV late at night, I'll hear advertisements for *first-time home buyer programs with no money down.*

There are a few programs that allow you to purchase a home with little to no money down.

There are even grants available to assist with a home purchase.

Some of the most common home loan programs with minimal down payment amounts today are with FHA loans, VA loans, and USDA loans.

Let me tell you a little bit about each one of these.

FHA Loans

FHA, which is short for Federal Housing Administration is a loan product for mortgages backed by the federal government. In essence, it works like insurance or a guarantee for mortgages, this allows lenders to reduce down payments on FHA mortgages to potential home buyers.

The FHA loans do have some limitations. The amount of the actual mortgage loan amount can vary, depending on where you live. There are caps on how expensive the home can actually be. You would want to research to see what the maximum loan amount is in your desired area.

I would quote the number for DFW here but it changes sometimes.

FHA mortgages require a small down payment of 3.5%. However, down payment assistance is often available to first-time home buyers when using the FHA loan.

Together, the FHA mortgage and the down payment assistance result in a zero-down mortgage. These can be a little complicated and tricky so seek out the knowledge of a professional when trying to figure out what you qualify for.

Down payment assistance programs are managed by your local government, if you qualify, they may cover the entire down payment for you. When I say local government entity, I'm referring to the city, town, or county you are buying the home in.

Depending on the program, the down payment may or may not need to be paid back over time.

Look into the city or the individual county that you're purchasing a home in for more information about their specific down payment assistance program. Each one is different.

VA Loans

A veteran, the surviving spouse of a veteran, or an active member of the military, should consider obtaining a mortgage through the Veterans Administration.

This is a great option for those who qualify.

A Certificate of Eligibility (COE) must be obtained before your application can begin. This process can be completed online at the Veterans Administration (VA) website, or by manually completing VA Form 26-1880, *Request for a Certificate of Eligibility* and mailing it to the VA Eligibility Center. To find more information about the eligibility requirements, visit http://www.benefits.va.gov/homeloans

Once you've obtained your COE, the rest of the process is similar to that of any other mortgage, but you don't need perfect credit to qualify.

Your lender would guide you through this process.

USDA Loans

The United States Department of Agriculture (USDA) mortgage is another government-backed and no-money-down option.

The program is a 100% financed mortgage and is used to assist people to buy homes in rural areas. The way DFW is growing, you'd be surprised which homes actually qualify for USDA loans.

The Metroplex is expanding and some areas that were previously considered *rural*, are attracting more and more first time homebuyers.

The home must be in a "USDA-defined" area to qualify. However, that doesn't mean the homes have to be out in the middle of nowhere.

Often, the physical boundaries of the location may include portions of suburban DFW. We don't see many of these in the city of Dallas but in other areas of the Metroplex, they do exist.

If you want to check to see if a home is USDA eligible, visit this website http://eligibility.sc.egov.usda.gov

Purchasing a home with no money down is a goal for many people, as it should be. Who wants to pay if they don't have to?

Zero-down mortgages are not easily found as they were years ago, but they do exist.

Home ownership is not out of reach because you don't have a large down payment accumulating in your bank account right now.

Be smart. If it's not the right time financially to buy a home, then don't.

The best way to find out what programs you would qualify for would be to speak with a lender. Again, these programs all have different requirements so like I said earlier, get educated.

Some of these programs have credit requirements; some have income restrictions.

Some may be location based, some vary by the type of home you are purchasing.

There are many things to consider with down payment assistance programs. Think about how your monthly payment can differ when you don't put any more down.

You need to make sure it will really be worth it to you.

BONUS: CHAPTER ELEVEN

How Much Money Do Real Estate Agents Make?

I'm not sure if you have seen any of my videos on YouTube yet, if not, go and check them out. I have a whole channel full.

I recorded a video some time ago and titled it "How Much Money do Real Estate Agents Make?" Let me tell you, that video went viral. I was pretty surprised at how many people were actually interested in this. I'm pretty sure it's because of the real estate shows people see on TV, but still!

I am continuously shocked, to this day, how many views this video has received. It's by far my most popular video with tens of thousands of views. I know that's not the biggest number of YouTube views but it sure was big for me.

Let me start off by saying, most real estate agents are commissioned sales people. This is a commissioned career.

I'm sure you know what that means but if not, it simply means if we don't sell, we don't get paid.

If an agent does not get clients and help them buy or sell homes, they don't eat. As an agent, I do not have a salary nor can I be guaranteed when my next check will be, nothing is guaranteed in this business.

I know you are probably thinking about the big agent commissions that you see on TV. Let me say, yes those do exist. But, you must also understand, those agents work very hard for their money.

According to NAR (National Association of Realtors®), the median gross income for agents was

$45,800 in 2014. Let me break down a little bit how the commission structure works when it comes to real estate.

In Texas, the typical commission for a sale is 6% of the sales price. So as an example, if a home sells for $150,000, the commission is $9,000. [$150,000 x .06)

That sounds like a good chunk of change right? With that, someone can probably get them something really nice and extravagant. Or maybe even not work for a couple of months. Well, stay with me here.

During most real estate transactions, there are 2 different parties involved. There's the buyer and there's the seller. I'm sure by now you knew that already. Well each side has their own agent that has to get paid out of the deal. Guess what that means... yes, the commission is split in half. This is noted in most listing agreements for sellers to see.

Now, if my calculations are correct, each side receives $4,500. Each side is inclusive of the broker who is paid next. In Texas, all salespeople are required to have their license held by a broker and work under a broker. The broker is the big liable responsible party for the agents. Brokers have splits. The split is what the broker keeps in a transaction and what an agent keeps in a transaction. There's no magic number for the split that an agent may have with their broker.

Some may have a 50/50 split, some may have a 100% split, or anything in-between. That means the agent would keep 50% of the $4,500 and the broker would keep the other 50%. On a 50/50 split, the agent takes home $2,250.

Still with me? So far we have accounted for both sides of the transaction and the brokers split. Unfortunately, that's not it. Since we are in the United States of America and commissions are income, you know what comes next…taxes.

Taxes have to be paid, each year. Along with insurance and anything else that the government requires us to have these days.

Want to know how much a real estate agent makes? I'm sure you have a general idea by now. The reason I say this is because I often speak with sellers and buyers that ask for reduced commissions or rebates. Basically, they are asking the agent to pay them for doing their job.

I'm a pretty understanding person and I can't fault someone for not knowing exactly what an agent makes or will make from a transaction, but that question really makes me cringe.

Since real estate is a commissioned position, nothing is guaranteed. So, just a bit of advice, before you decide to talk down your agent or ask for money back, just think about what they may have to pay for out of the money they will receive for doing their job. You never know what someone has going on or who or what they have to support in their life. Don't discount your agent. If you feel that their services were not as they promised, that's a different discussion. But to discount an agent just for the heck of it, that's just inconsiderate if you ask me.

I explain all of this a bit more in my video. You should still check it out. As a matter of fact, I have a few videos on my channel speaking about different areas of the actual career of the real estate agent. They're pretty interesting.

If it's something that interests you, go and check it out. Leave me feedback on what you think of them.

The rewards can be extremely beneficial in this business, but one must work hard. It does not come easy. If you read my story earlier in the book, I moved here from a different city. Heck, a different state. I had to start, establish, and build a real estate business.

Every day is a new learning experience.

Every day is a new challenge.

Every day is a new opportunity.

Every day is a new beginning.

I embrace them and I am grateful for them. I thank God everyday for allowing me to serve this world everyday with my talents that he has given me.

Something my good friend Rogers tells me often is "*enjoy the journey*," and I can say, this real estate journey is bringing me great joy.

This is the end of my book. Thank you for reading it. If you have learned at least one thing, I have done what I intended to do. If not, I know that there is someone you know that would learn something. Get them a copy.

Now, our relationship is established.
Let's continue to grow it.

Contact Me

Chastin J. Miles

Rogers Healy and Associates

Phone: 214-589-0096

cmiles@chastinjmiles.com

chastinjmiles.com

www.ingramcontent.com/pod-product-compliance
Lightning Source LLC
Chambersburg PA
CBHW072214170526
45158CB00002BA/596